The Crooked Beak of Love

The CROOKED
BEAK of LOVE

Duane Niatum

WEST END PRESS

Acknowledgments

The poems in this book originally appeared in the following
publications whose editors I would like to thank: *Albatross,
The Amicus Journal, Archae, Calapooya, Caliban, The Charitan
Review, Chelsea, Chrysanthemum, Contact II, Crab Creek Review,
Jeopardy, Left Bank, North Dakota Quarterly, Potlatch, Princeton
Spectrum, Seattle Arts, Seattle Review, Spring Rain,* and *Talus.*
"Skagit Valley" originally appeared in *Ascending Red Cedar Moon*
under the title "The Rhythm." "His Medicine Man" originally
appeared in *Digging Out the Roots* under the title "His Teacher."
An earlier version of "Crow's Fear of Growing White" originally
appeared in *Songs for the Harvester of Dreams.* "Stories of the
Moon" originally appeared in *Ascending Red Cedar Moon*
under the title "Legends of the Moons."

First edition, February 2000.
ISBN: 0-931122-96-1

Book and cover design by Nancy Woodard

Distributed by University of New Mexico Press

West End Press • P.O. Box 27334 • Albuquerque, New Mexico 87125

To those friends who have supported me in my pursuit of art.

Books by Duane Niatum

Drawings of the Song Animals: New and Selected Poems, 1991
Songs for the Harvester of Dreams, 1981
Digging Out the Roots, 1977
Ascending Red Cedar Moon, 1974
After the Death of an Elder Klallam, 1970

EDITOR
*Harper's Anthology of 20th Century Native American
 Poetry,* 1988
Carriers of the Dream Wheel, 1975

CONTENTS

Preface

I want it to be known that I have never pretended to be a voice other than what I am. From the beginning of my writing career, I realized after reading many of the books by American Indians and attending many art exhibits that American Indian literature and art call for multiple voices, and mine is only one from the community.

Since I was born and raised largely in the city, I do not consider myself a spokesman for reservation Indians. But because my Klallam grandfather's values are essentially my own, my life and art will always resonate to some degree with those beliefs. These could be the strongest ties I have to the traditional world of the American Indian.

My aesthetic position has always been to learn and grow from whatever sources of knowledge were available. I have, without exception, believed it extremely important to maintain a balance and give my reader the wholeness of my experience through living in both worlds. Fortunately, time has shown me how to live within this paradox. Art continues to offer the opportunity of surviving in both worlds no matter how challenging that may become at times.

Upon first reading, some of my poems such as "December Rose" and "Rufous Hummingbird" might seem to have little connection to the Indian side of my being, but believe me, most do. On the other hand, one poem that easily reflects this connection is "Song of the Yellow Pine," a poem honoring the last of the basket makers in my family. The poem goes back to my childhood when I spent time living with my grandfather and other members of our family who lived in a house that he built in Hadlock.

My grandfather's life and stories became the touchstones of my life and art. The center of my artistic self starts from his home and his parents' home which was almost on the beach. Therefore, my grandfather's place of ancestors will go on shaping and nourishing my life and art to the grave. Perhaps the greatest gift his presence gave me was a strong sense that I could resist, in my own way, the destructive forces of mainstream culture. However, I do not feel this requires that I sever myself completely from white culture. That would be like thinking it necessary to sever my right hand with my left one. As a mixed-blood such an act would be a physical and spiritual suicide. Rather, I believe it would be in our artistic community's interest to utilize what is best in both cultures and attempt to heal the old, old wounds, with reciprocity being an inherent part of the healing.

It also seems necessary to point out to the reader of this volume that a number of the poems that appeared in earlier volumes of my work have been revised so extensively that they have become mere shells of their former selves. For example, the poems from a moon cycle that appeared in *Ascending Red Cedar Moon* have not been simply recycled to fit a new context, but have been re-composed to such a degree that they are really new works made from old parts. The revisions have resulted in changing the contents, and I would be the first to admit this is the case with a few others as well. These changes reflect my effort to profit from my mistakes and include material that should not have been omitted.

The five sections of this book have been presented more by theme than chronological order. The poems within each section were also arranged in a more congenial sequence, regardless of whether they were composed in that order. I would like to thank Gayle Bodorff and Nelson Bentley for reading the drafts of the manuscript and making thoughtful suggestions. Gayle also helped give order and shape to the book's form.

I
FIRST PEOPLE

Crow's Fear of Growing White

When I can no longer see
the elders by firelight in the villages
still wrapped in a song blanket,
when son, daughter, mother and father
stop talking with the red cedar,
when the last woman quits beating
her guardian hummingbird to earth,
when a fisherman eats his greed
until his bones shatter before the eyes
of the disappearing sockeye salmon,
when the tribes stop believing their destroyers,
when the seal that gave my youth
a shield of dream circles tells
me no more stories of the sea,
and blue jay warns not even the ants
of the next storm, only then will
Crow end his fear of growing white.

His Medicine Man

The bone comedian jumps right out
of the dream to lurk before my bed;

steps north and south, east and west;
his clapper whirrs like a legless wasp.

After knocking the window to pieces,
he clubs the bedpost that echoes

through each room, Old Grease Bowl,
the uninvited Trickster, as if it were

his sacred smokehouse and I an alien.
He acts as coy as a former love who

just called, asking how is my love life
and do I need a back rub. I groaned,

swore a little, dropped the phone,
turned left, then right, then over.

So not to appear off the forked path,
lost, baiting the wrong field mouse,

my teacher taps my bedpost
four times with his fanged rattle,

accusing me of not paying attention,
then goads me into facing the dancers,

Otter Running Mouth, Mosquito Mocking Scab,
Muscatel's Knee Stump, Cancer's vigilantes,

pain's tribe of giants wreathed
in stinger nettles, kelp, jelly fish and sand fleas.

Bored with his refusal to see his latest
hat of fears was accepted decades ago,

I try to shame Big Stink Claw
with my own death bundle;

my one crow clapper to earn
the slow burn. I declare wearing

my own Changer mask that if
the wily wizard doesn't jump

from my bedroom into someone
else's jumping dream, I will.

To seize the moment from the clown
exposing my scars to the stars

and moon, our ancestors, I toss
their necklace to the bear comedian,

the one faking promises of sunlight,
the one turning me loose in a new fog blanket.

Days We Need a Good Rain

Days that run away from home,
nights that turn the chairs into vampires,
days when history and the siren
are buried in the archives of the heart,
we need a good rain to open
our eyes and bring us back to life.

These are days we need a downpour
to wake the sense passed out beside the toilet,
its dream of cherry blossoms growing
through the window, near the stairs
where the door used to be—a house, a spirit,

when the mind didn't even know
it had a voice or a grave, and the body
said no more blackouts, enough already,
enough, enough,—O, could we use
a little raincatcher.

Days pure stencils of memory
when we ask the skeletons to quit
fancy dancing; remind them that Pow Wow
ended years ago, and the drums
and whistles and feathers are in the van
in the ditch, on the margin west

of the cowboys and east of the cows,
the last reservation anybody found
with a pony, a bottle, a BIA flag,
a sheriff's handcuffs, a Pay N. Save shaman.
O, those are the days for rain.

The days we welcome a good rain
parched lips need soothing,
chattering teeth need capping,   .
healing words need a comma
or a scene of a world beyond
the white man's purple sunset.
On these days we are certain
to feel the legs buckle for a little rain.

Days the animals vanish in saran wrap,
the delirium truck stalls at the razor's edge,
after doing the whole race in reverse,
on the wrong course with no sign
of where the right turn was left,

or when any of it will end,
on days when the blackberry
brier whiskey seer shakes his staff
for mom and dad, brother and sister,
aunt and uncle, cousin and cat,
to step lively down the vomit path,
we will need a downpour.

Song of Breath and Water

Ojibwa grandmother,
shawl of hunter, fisherman and dreamer;
the inner-flow and weave of yellow-green-brown
calls the Nishnaabeg from sleep
to birth dance, step with wind, rice
in the footprints of moon,
hear deer and beaver jump from fire,
fish leap from stream and lake onto Turtle's back,
the island spinning like the conjuring lodge.

The heart's wintergreen,
medicine woman of spruce and sun;
with eyes closed you are the river of fire,
lake and stream between dawn and night,
bush where blue quail huddle from the fox,
snow bell breaking through ice,
den of Muskrat during storms,
lodge of the four winds,
music in words the color of icicles.

Moon's harvester,
carrier of turquoise, sweet grass and turtle's shell,
you hold four seasons in your hands
like a basket of blueberries.
Sky single-stitches a slope of sunflowers
within reach of any child
picking blossoms for the hair
of a mother or grandmother or great grandmother
and the first dream visitor from the forest.

Daughter of Maple Sugar Moon,
you welcome children and travelers
to the feast of first fruits.
Voices of the chi-ah-ya-og flow
from the water drum to bless the feast.
Daughter of the moon answers the elders
like sparks of chipped flint.
Sun opens its mouth, a stone in her hand.

Ojibwa grandmother
taps the corn grinding stone seven times
for grandfathers, golden eagles hovering
below the stratus clouds passing on the wind.
North Star looks down at the road
gravity formed, the moss-edged side—
home of mushroom and frog, weeping willow,
trunk and food run for the red-breasted nuthatch.
Sky Bear keeps the people's bundle
in his paws, dream path of the Nishnaabeg.
Grandmother sings in and out of every storm,
every crack in the settlement's vein and marrow.

November Watercolor

On Earthmother's bird-bone path
the sun spills its orange light over frozen hills.
The last chrysanthemum glistens with frost pollen.
Underneath all this change from warm to chill
is a faint tint of sun, pink as peeling birch bark.
By early evening the cold returns,
rises from the sidewalk and grass like a mist,
plays with the wind direction.
Objects drop from view on the path
to your window. Your memory fills in
the vanishing point with old stories,
blood tracks down beauty's field.

Yet the scent and pout of the thistle-queen
you met at a Pow Wow lingers in your nostrils
and on your fingers.
You asked her to round-dance with you
for the moon's blessing but she chose
someone else to dangle like a key,
proving what you guessed, great odds
against a rainbow-throbbing night
in such a woman's nest woven to lightning-bolts.
When you later met a younger woman
with spiked boots in protest, you
nearly lost your arrow's flight.
So you left those walls pressing in
to cross the lake where last summer frogs
eyed you like a grandparent.

You pick a few remains of thyme,
rosemary, and sage from the field,
bouquets strewn about the land
of the Great Lakes; their petals
shine as stiff as stone. The field
exudes fragrances the wood lice wonder
at biting, sniffing, bedding down in.

The sky is a vacancy of hunters and warriors;
its rhythms fall as sacked as the season.
Earthmother winks and sways in her shawl
over the land and people, rocking in her embrace.
You wish she was the thistle-queen.
She shakes the flakes from her skirt;

ermine shadows soften the winter dance.
Her lust shines like the snow wash she creates.
Rays reflect the minnow surge of the river
seen through a cattail reed.
She leaves wearing her barb and bristle look
and you can almost hear the thistle-queen's
parting shot, "I may choose you or sweat
alone with sweet grass and my dreams.
I'm from the Wolf clan and during famines
we ate ravens and crows."

Earthmother crosses the river,
her step as graceful as the heron's.
She beckons you with her
eagle-feather fan to hear obsidian stories
of her day and night flights
through the star quilt, what tribes
are left on Turtle's back,
this rootbelly of rosehip and corn tassel.

But from the maples North Wind
suggests you keep moving like the muddy-
mouthed crows feeding their shadows
sky kernels. When you reach the porch
and the wind is less than a yawn,
your potted downy-yellow violets,
gift of the thistle-queen whose dance
turned as cold as snow on linoleum,
fly out the window to trade obsession for air.

Song of the Yellow Pine

When death takes another parent
from our arms, Oatsa's song basket keeps
my cousins and myself returning
to this Hadlock cliff that was the home
of Young and Lucy Patsy,
our great grandparents.
Before the dusk claims our hearts
we burn red cedar in their name;
build a fire to hear the wind
change the stars into Oatsa's stories
of "Thunderbird and Crow,"
"A Young Woman Marries a Sea Being."

Tomorrow at break of day
we'll stand on the bank of Chemakum Creek
to see the story in the basket
show the ways the creek lured
tyee salmon with the counter-motions
of their gravel garden.

To honor the shadow people
who bring us our songs in dreams,
we dance down the hill and wait
for the fire to spark and light the sky
with Oatsa's awl weaving our lives
into the story of the day her grandchildren
picked chokecherries until darkness
took away the path, the day
she teased her husband, Niatum.
Our great grandpa stood on the cliff's
edge swinging his cane at us
who stole his canoe to paddle beyond
the gray willow swish of his anger,
the cackle of the crows and herring gulls
swaying in the wind to his rage.
Then they returned to catching
the black cherries we tossed in the air
and continued gliding around our heads
on a stream above Skunk Island.

To Our Salish Women Who Weave the Seasons
(for Mary Peters)

I try to sleep
on a tule mat to see what the dream

shows of the last Klallam grandmother
to weave such bulrush grass. I drop

a red cedar wreath
into the Hoko River to put the family ghosts

to bed. Grandmother weavers often circle
our struggles, come to witness people falling

out of their skins,
nourish those shaking with disease or madness,

soften our yoke to the years-wheel. The stories
carved on the elders' staff of my nomadic

pantomime live on only
when the spindle whorls dance. How do

I speak with these women in bark capes
and hats who spin in

and out of my life like a wedding on fire? How
reach the hands of these elders the Transformer

promised a healing path
out of darkness and despair so the words of our

storyteller would always be caught in the sunstone's
net, at the long pauses of the short notes?

These women clack
humor-rattles and teach us the power of laughter

to switch the lights back on, soothe our fears,
tie our family and the villages to the center

of the basket. They taunt
enemies into self-destruction before our ancestral

mountains the ravagers have made as barren
as the backs of mangy dogs. O these

       sea and river weavers
hum and sing until our grief turns to laughter

on Crow's mirror. They tell me in their own
snow-water voices—sing morning and night

       to Crow, first basket
maker before his baskets became clamshell gifts—

so by the next moon the sun will pluck the heart's
guitar. O these women in Thunderbird and Wolf

       capes let me know
when I'm up to my neck in rapids, I'm at home

and a son of their tribe as mutilated as the earth,
but still half osprey and half salmon.

       So every bone that wants
to sing—sings; every nerve that wants to burn—burns.

Awe-Shaker

Night tracker changes our days
and the path before us as we go

backwards to go forward. It feathers
the storm and digs the lime holes

we sooner or later fill the earth with.
It does its muddy-toe dance from the mirror

so the wind echoes rain, bone, and ice.
Awe-shaker is no clown when time seizes

a young girl, grandmother, or opossum,
spoiling their chances of carving

a leaping-back stick to touch sun's poppy.
It sends side-glance waves of moon needles

to have us guess what stars are singing;
sometimes tree-barks from the quantum edge

that holds our feet on the ground like an earthquake.
O our awe-grinning marvel—masked and unmasked—

night raven, pinches our hearts so we drop like snowberries.

Muskogee Carrier of the Stories
(for Louis Little Racoon Oliver, 1904–1991)

We will always find Louis at Koweta Town,
sitting before the fire, waiting for those
who come from the stars to tell the ancient
stories. Louis learned from the Old Ones
that Yahola, first teacher of the Creeks,
came to offer the story of the ball of fire
and red seed arrow the people can follow
day and night. Yahola said to walk in
the direction of the arrow, his gift
to the seven clans, keep to the sun's path.

From memory's cave Louis built the Bighouse,
Chukomako, out of rock and cedar
and sage and pitch, out of love
for his grandmother and aunts who told him
of the ball of fire, the birthplace
of his clan, the way to burn the sacred wood:
sycamore, cane and elm.

His grandmother spoke of how their home
began at Chatahoche, rock of the elders.
Tekapay'cha circled the fire
until the birthplace of her grandson's yearning
flew back to its badger's burrow,
turtle tracks under red and yellow willow
on the banks of the Okmulgee River.

He played the flute for his aunts
who stomp danced around him; asked their
musician please bring the night and morning
sun into their hearts; chew and swallow
history and defeat like the roots
they will soon make into tea. His grandmother
heard from the mountain spirits that Louis
brought his aunts the kindling for the dawn song.
His aunts gave him an herb potion,
the gift that would build new life
from the chipped-flint of the people's sorrow;
they sprinkled sage into the fire and sang
of the star people leading to the Chukomako,
the Bighouse where in the shadow of Racoon,
the sacred fire returns the people
to the deepest river of earth and mind.

His aunts told him it was the trail of blood,
the four steady points of the heart,
the gift of ancestors that fills the night
with light. They remind him of the story
when he was a child that the enemy
wears so many masks and words
as hollow as reeds that he must learn
the language of herbs and trees,
catfish and trout, wolf and deer,
squirrel and bear, bee and butterfly,
so not to be betrayed
by their diseased language.

He painted the figures of his dreams
on animal skins and visited the sweatlodge
the days no sun rose from its yellow basket.
Nights his voice abandoned him
the ancestors sang little more than stars.
Silence was an empty grave;
ancestors refused to tell where
to trade bones for new directions,
scars for a drop of water on the tongue,
confusions for hummingbird's song.
He then danced for green corn and sanity
and another fire ceremony.

His grandmother leaned back into shadow
in the opposite direction to fool
the Little People who might trick his dreams.
She said stand like Thunder Being
even if a wing catches fire in a wind rage
over the deaths of so many guardians
of the people's path, the animals carrying
in their backbones the seasoned drums
of stone, feast and story.

Little Raccoon stokes the fire and hums
to its people; we hear the blanket stories
build a path to a lodge beyond pain,
the sacked villages and towns,
the voices trapped in treeless darkness, the body
tearing itself from the dream-wheel's home.

O listen inwardly, listen to your own voice
form a swallow flight, a rainbow over the ruins.
O watch the night people change
the round dance of light.

Find your path, the lightning snake's!

Raven the Great Toe Word Clacker

The old red cedar speaks
of dances and feasts, birth,
death, and laughter.

Each voice of the dream wheel
plays a part in old cedar's song
beating the promise wings

in your age continually cracking,
slipping from eye and mind,
dawn and dusk's blue bruises.

Yet Raven is the mask master,
irony's gift in your love's eye,
bringing to the scene tossed light

to warm the shadow drifts
of your death defiant dance.
You witness now and forever

the grave's merry markers, what
shows spikier fictions than those
streaming through the window,

the backward painted stories of stars.
What bird flies over your head
to disappear before the clouds

is not flying for the future,
nor for your tight-jawed past,
but the snow-wrapped mountain

buried in plastic and chemical mounds.
So follow the wind voices
through the council of yellow leaves,

the cold nights burdened with your lies.
You will remember the child you lost,
the night peeling you down to your

irascible, unknowing impulses and itches.
Love the blindness that names you,
the feelings wound around your heart

like a rope, misplaced, awkward,
and as receding as the day's
philosophy of sunlight. So honor

the night's paintings of feast and famine,
one toe clapping for happy moments,
one finger bent backward in sadness,

your undercover sexual frenzy rides,
life in and out of inconstant boxes.
Don't snap like a twig at the constant

alarm of the door swinging open
to natural and unnatural movements and breaths,
the self-delusive acts of what you dreamed.

See beyond the over- and under-exposed
photos; search for the family remains
fallen between the cracks of memory.

We Sing in this Life so the Dead Come Home

I. Ancestors

As a child I hid
from my ancestors when the enemy
was myself. No one heard Crow laugh
the many times I tripped and hit the dirt
on the path through the black ravine.

I was a boy who wandered in footprints
that vanished with sand and tide.
The moon rose all evening writing
her song that brought the mountains close;
the surf rolled up and down
while the moon shook her rattle and danced.

One night in my grandfather's house
the wind banged and bellowed the half-opened
window. I heard in the dark
it would take three runs down the night
for the shape-changing shadows
to become what dream carriers last.
When I fell asleep on the beach
I dreamt a seal brought me a drum
and a song that would soothe my nerves.
Seal said my life would be formed by the sea
but I would know this mother mostly by land.

One morning when I was sitting down to talk
with the red cedars, an ancestor with elkhorn flute
sent notes dancing above the beach fire
of the Patsy clan the story of Wolf
who called the sun to pull us from the heart's war.

II. Gifts

Mother Spruce taught the many loops path
of the dream's arrow. She showed how to laugh
even when the battle cry was uttered by
my own voice. She said my footprint
was the quicksand enemy when I could not name
my family in the forest, sea, or sky. Until
my song rose to the mountains
with eagle and osprey I should leave
no tracks to chance.

Mother Spruce sang in the wind
that the Fire Dancers will offer a new path
when the One-Who-Loathes-Too-Much snares
the heart with a new disaster. She
said the cave of the Fire Dancers
throws light on youth's green death.

III. Old Man

My grandfather was at the Elwha River
when the dams cut her off from her children.
The days and nights and seasons flow
into the banks of our lives but the river
never regained her family voices.
With the years as his talking sticks,
Old Man showed us the path
of wind, kingfisher, cattail, and river.
We see him always as the red willow
who walks as steady as the rising sun.
My grandfather takes me back
to where he tossed his last net into pools
swirling with the fins of salmon.
Chickadees were feeding there
on pine nut offerings; dragonflies were there
for the water in the shadow dance.

IV. Visits to Neah Bay

The Makah gather each summer
to let Song-maker loose again; to bring children
the circle of their ancestors
who weave a sunlight blanket.
A sacred clown, Song-maker rainbows
the cape and village with fire and dance.
He welcomes the people to feast on salmon,
clams, oysters, corn and tuk.
For a few hours the people of the cape
are a round-dance of happiness
while the sea carves their paddles into Wolf,
Grizzly Bear and Eagle. Children
ride on the blanket until the tide chases
them into the arms of grandparents.

In the evening breakers, the sun cools.
Drums strike a chord even in the heart of Raven;
Raven dances the whale hunt for the children.
The dance speaks of when their fathers',
fathers', fathers roamed the coast in canoes
carved out of joy for the hunt, and tonight
draw what family survives to pitch their losses
and griefs on the fire, live in the weave
of elder, shell and bone. Now that I join
the circle of grandparents, my son
hears their story and why this ceremony
keeps our toes close to whales,
our eyes to fishhawks and bald eagles.

Son, This is What I Can Tell You

Time, the mapmaker and the one who peppers
the road with holes deeper than a thunder's crack,
the clown who laughs or cries in the tunnel
by which we stumble until it offers oblivion,
grows louder than the madness drums
as we grow smaller and deafer.

O yes, in my vanity and pride I was nourished
like the water ouzel on the iced, tart-red punch
of The-One-Who-Knows-but-Never-Tells.

This is the hurdle that will test your bones
and mind as well as spirit: nothing
during these forty-eight years hinted how
the minutes, days, decades can be stopped
from slipping through our fingers like jelly
as we drift into absence. For what lights
the future to the past is blacker
than Killer Whale's fin and as indifferent
to our story as our birth.

And just the other night I picked myself up
from a fall as slow as a face focusing on a yellow
photograph, yet lighter than a dragonfly's wing.
Standing in that darkness I heard for the first time
the bird that chanted from my ribcage
an answer to death: not yet, not yet.
Son, its voice hummed a reality more present
than the people and art discovered in the city,
country, sky, sea, river, and heart.

These figures change our lives, the puzzle,
shape, color, direction, and name what
we see before they can live with our ashes
or their own. So the seasons show the way
to drop into ourselves like the turtle
on its back, to want merely the half-notes
of Venus and the stars, to be the remains
of night, its dancer dangling
from the sky's daisy-chain web.

And like your mother's, there's a woman's embrace,
nature, the arts and the shield of love.
I loved your mother because she gave me a gift—
you, and the will to be soft and not cruel,

a man and not a machine, a failure
but a carrier of the moon's blue basket of sky.
Your gentle mother set loose a song sparrow that flew
through my sleep's evergreens.
From such a field I believe the diamond-cutting
fiction of a rising sun.

So, my son who takes a different road
away from the red cedar and yellow pine,
the road that brings me to my gnarled elders,
the earth and shore of my Klallam family—
try to remember when your anger lifts
like a fog from a coastal storm,
I cannot call you back, cannot offer what
was not theirs, nor mine, the popping fire
and butterfly dance of this land.

When you roll like riverbed gravel,
fall like the sun through Red-flowering currant,
see more as the feather than antler,
you will find that the bald eagle and salmon,
forest and sea can call you back.
Nature is the one who carves the way to unravel
the spine's four knots. Then the wounds I gave you
as a child will drop like mountain rain
into my opened hands. For your father was seasoned
on salt air and the longhouse stories
and a life it takes blood rage to appease.

II
WINDOWS

This Spring the Finch Is Songmaker

Outside the window his voice
speaks of the slow path of the sun;
asks primroses to rise and dance.
The moment's warmth lightens
the nest with fragrant red cedar.

From notecatcher
to the morning's braids,
the sun has burrowed like a woodpecker
into so many birth pulses rain
is almost dry. The day rocks like
an accidental reflex in the prism
of each direction.

The air holds for one
chord from the finch's breast
vibrating with sky spirits:
deaths, faces, words trudging
their way back to caves.

Dogs answer police and ambulance sirens.
The finch with burnt-orange cap
sings through the horn of discordancy.
Hearing notes open my skin
to its breath lines, how could
I fail to lie like an unraveled knot
in a nest with these birds,
the better part of my family?

Windows

He often looks out windows
to catch drizzle-clouds breaking apart
like snowberries, beyond his history
scrambled and as fine as raven dust
scattering the year's defeats
the four directions of the wind.

He grows lighter touching earth,
for there among the vines and robins
and worms was the steady rain last week,
the bulbous sun today, rising from the lake
to color the trees in ocher shadow,
reach their inner cells, still half asleep,
and his, the blood at his spine's base.

He learns how to fly by looking out windows
at the world removed from his mind's net,
for it is the titmouse hanging
topsy-turvy on the maple branch, perhaps,
the crocus band appearing at his door,
the cherry tree, as knurled as Seattle,
that his recent deaths cannot inherit.

The Washington Park Arboretum

Within the lazy drifts of cattails,
two mallards doze, drunker than the sun.
A dragonfly is as translucent
as the lily pad it has pinned itself to;
a swallow-tailed butterfly, the path's
amulet, disappears in the reeds;
Summer's farewell dangles like dusk.
Ready to walk into this painting
I step closer to the white-edged water
turning to smoke, touch the bottom
of the lake, slip from my shadow.

Survival Song at Fifty

Since my heart learns to rock
to the end of its own creek
like a Coho salmon before a fish-ladder,
I ignore my face, wine-speckled
as mirror lice, decide it is better
to live with an empty book
than memories that never make it
back to river gravel.

The day's floral run slopes
down the wall opposite the window.
Like the music it flows over the daisy,
my favorite joker from the field;
this flower stands as solitary as the vase
so formed to light change, the push
and pull of earth and piano; it needs
no color, forest, or sky, only its mask
dancing with the petals falling
to the floor over Chopin nocturnes.

But the purple violet would have
been this week's flower if it was not
the soul of John Keats, my mentor
who drank with the gods
for imagination and truth, the life
that sometimes flings us head first
into the ditch to flake like stone,
lustless and sweatless as stars,
sometimes adorns us with a handful of roses
to step like Orpheus into the pool of night.

To Nelson Bentley Who Praised the Figures
Born of Sensation

In the midst of the white swirl
round and round the seven hills of Seattle,
the North wind gusting to 78 miles per hour,
a friend calls to tell our poet-teacher is dead.
The news, like the storm, loops
through the apartment half the night,
the book I can no longer read,
music no longer hear. This addition
joins the other losses blocking out
the fleshless, clearcut moon.

The wind riddles its chords and discords
from branch to house to door, what
laurel, maple and madrona remain standing.
Whipping its way across the state, it hints
"Don't be too sure this isn't Nome,
Alaska, or Grand Folks, North Dakota;
don't be surprised if the icicle bear
reduces what the windows frame to comic reliefs."
Like my Salish elders and the zen monks,
you turn the scene into a drinking song.

Wanting to follow your humor
in these rooms closing down in darkness,
I dance on one foot to feel how
our branches break, roots shrink
and divide like memories, how we are more
abstract figures than present at the births
of sensation, whether within our blood
or from the galaxies, how bound like grubs
in the labyrinth of dying. Still, you
smile and translate the eternal laughter.

Now that your spirit wanders the roads
and paths, the fields to forest and sea,
you glance sideways and speak of other journeys
while sparrows bank into the infinite,
sandpipers bounce like shells in the surf.
You play the storm rhythms before turning
yourself into a light figure at dark's periphery,
submit to the sea's claim;
you who said she was the first
to create our words from sand and tide.

III
LOVE CHANGES THE SPIRIT AND THE DANCE

Skagit Valley

A woman and I
follow the bend
in the river
valley for miles;
slip into each
other's shadow
like the heron
in the current;
its banks speckle
the earth like trout.

I turn in circles
and toss a stone;
it hums with the poplars,
bounces four strands
of water before
a flake of sunrise.
Our ears are hills
in which gold echoes
of light fall home.

A few animals
still reach the forest
in the Changer's tracks.
From these tracks the Skagits
once lit morning fires
at the mouth
of the Nooksack river.

Komo Kulshan,
the white steep watcher
above the red-tailed
hawk on the spruce-top,
is grandfather
of thaw and thistle.

By sunset we dance
with the Lummi,
the Swinomish,
the brake and deer fern,
willow and wild rose,
learn to touch
like the madrona leaves,
unravel like moonlight.

Moonrise at Oak Bay

We lie in the sand to blend in;
you shape from clay the moon's necklace,
pinch out of her the August night's
abalone sheen, a path to match
the bear-grass dunes of the sky.

Our shadows are coots floating
in the ebb and flow of lineage.
Your eyes skim over the sparks the reunion
drum-stomps into our moccasins.
I warned you my family holds together
like sawdust board in a winter gale.

You see generations of Klallams shake
and scatter like their subtracted history;
already quarrels filled the day
with the smashed bottles of old feuds.
From one shoulderless end of the beach
to the other, everyone jokes
to feather the evasion.

When my soul quiets down from the seizure,
we huddle under a blanket leaning
for the far country of the next county;
write in the sand that we will leave
these ashes on the morning tide.

Love Changed Our Spirits and the Dance

I

Feeling love's stitches fray apart
is like watching termites eat

through the door, the surprise
finding my words created such distress.

When you ran from the house
and I searched for you in the streets,

autumn frost collected in my teeth.
The intention of that letter

was that you receive
a quiet room of your own

to leave behind the unleashed fear.
You said on slamming the door:

"I feel like I'm living in five
nightmares at once." I replied:

"Where bury this tiny death of ours?"
You didn't answer and we froze

like snapshots in the rush of an avalanche.
Time sculptured us in the unsettled

battle and gravity shook the earth obtuse,
while light carved our faces into masks.

II

I took a long walk through one
of your nightmares recently.

The herring gull with broken wing
we saw on the beach rested its confidence

in the pit of my stomach—
I can still see its eyes telling me

I'm the only one who will help—
a goading apprehension neither had

the voice to accept or deny. You
don't know I went back to look

for the bird the next day and it was dead.
So I take your wounds into my heart

that were mirrored in the eye
of that dying bird: this other reality

falls as pointless as the stars:
the amorality of children,

the ageless cruelty of their jests.
Yet we, their parents, only differ

in seeing pain is the tapeworm
of the soul. We don't stone birds

or nail fish to a tree, but worse—
throw words at each other like stones;

assume these blackout figures
were not our own creations.

So please come back from the night,
let your steps light the vacancy,

tell me if you will, if our hands
never shook at each edge we spin to,

would our courage leap back
from the dark, from then to now?

A Moment of Recollection
(for Natalie)

You have become Euterpe, Mnemosyne's green-eyed
daughter who lounges in the unused study
of my mind. Yet your chance reappearance is not
nostalgic, but a sign of your tenderness.
Like the sixteen years it will pass.
We were bound more by dance than earth.

You broadened then focused my field.
No woman before suggested I sidestep fear,
break the childhood mirror, taste russet air.
You named the path that opened summer's gate
where storms were gut learned, little by heart.

You guessed winter has snow-paws
because the spirit takes us for joy
back over the old roads. It doesn't joke
to steal our sense of balance and proportion,
but as a guide through the best ruins.

So pretend we met and drank white Bordeaux,
imagine the other requested it by card
that states there will be music we once heard
when we weren't ready to juggle any more losses.
We came together like crossed winds
and parted like goslings on a wave of eelgrass.

Ode to the Daughter I Never Had

The day would surely arrive when the scents
of early evening would beckon us:
mock-orange, camellia, dogwood, hyacinth—
to touch their rainbow shapes and colors,
green-mouthed as the trout, a ripple of the river.

We might have stepped on into the night
where, from a madrona branch, a redwing
blackbird begins its reedy call so goose bumps
rise on our arms. For the magic,
we would have dangled our feet in the river.

One sunset would linger in the air—
a special waltz flickering harmonies down
the path to the wave, the moon and back.
We would draw in the mud with sticks
a starlight circle, a yellow friendship village

for our family and the animals on the road.
O slowly you would learn imagination
prunes our senses for falling to,
then rising from the earth. And a season
would follow when Ariadne, Homer, Keats,

Williams, Bogan would show you only fools,
claim there is no exit from the labyrinth.
Sappho and her musicians would name
the people, the statue-shells frozen
in what they mirror, those who always hide

from what dawn reaches by night.
Rain or shine, plague or rebirth, a cup
of beauty never makes them tight.
But their blindness and deafness is no matter.
For the lines you learned from memory

would help you hear Emily Dickinson
in her garden trading stories
with painters who translate the untranslated
pigments in space and time, life and death,
pain and decay, the mire of things unbindable.

O we would laugh each moment a storm bewildered
and hug like bears, so when you said goodbye,
it wouldn't echo ice. We would have caught
snow-buds with our tongues for pity's sake,
trumpeted the unknown and scorned the fake.

Mostly we would have talked
to the animals and the forest,
grateful as the dead to grow beside
the forget-me-nots and the other
exiles of the forest.

Chasing the Sun

We push away from the grass bank,
drier than the backs of grasshoppers.
Our canoe skims Lake Duwamish;
an arrow swishing into sunset.
With paddles in our hands
we race beyond the middle of our lives,
find a moment's certainty in the falling
beads of water. For countless strokes

blue dancers have leaped and twirled
along the white trail in the sky.
Keeping to the journey of great,
great grandparents, myths enter our singing.
We paddle in a figure eight to guard
their black expanse, join them dropping
above the lake's surface, as still
as a waxed crab-apple. If one chose
to dive in, surely the other would
and return to the surface as eternal
as the water lily, speaking
in petals to the sky dancers!

The Moves to Shrink the Distances
(for Rosa)

Bitter loves drove us into seclusion.
In youth we played long and hard
the sexual dances but learned in time
to throw away the music. This spring
we offer each other the slightly hoarse
heartbeats in the ballad,
the amusing motions of candlelight
each ignites in the other's eyes.
We step back into the world's whirlwinds,
open door and window on the dormant seasons;
our skin colors like Bacchus blooms.
What we make of hunger composes itself
with the stinging nettles of longing.
We never hid the desire of our hands
and fused the shadows and the blue notes
because the myths we acted out in early
dreams were carved into our souls
with Eros' arrows. Believing the interior
stars we tango out of clothes like butterflies
mating on an apple blossom branch—
two figures plunging into darkness,
the blind alley of pleasure.

In Your City of Stone, Sculpture and Ruin
(for Rosa)

You put my hand over your heart
and take me to Tiberina Island,
the place you said keeps your dreams
in a whirlpool of the Tiber.
You escape the moment like the river,
a beauty of Roma coveting a shield
from the soon to be departed.

You sense how the energy pulses
like a herd of Apollo's horses
through the muscles and veins
and will abandon you by twilight.
But today you pivot from the vacuum.
Cézanne would call you a modern Olympia;
I know you as a woman from the forest
of Fontainebleau who skipped down
the mountain path to pick
my heart like a persimmon.

The temples of your father's ancestors,
the Roman goddesses and their lusts
that changed the songs of half a dozen gods,
compose the steps you bring back
to earth. On day's rim, an orange-ocher
feast bowl, your body in a trance
turns the head of every stranger passing
us in the Piazza di Bocca della Verità
searching for the light that redeems ruins.

Born in the greenest folds of France,
your dark almond eyes trace from memory
the home that marks the healing ground
of our grandmother's circle,
the cypresses and willow, creatures
of the Seine River swimming and leaping
and diving past your grandparents'
house at Beaulieu.

Later, at the Piazza Navona, your hands
curl round your head, draw me to you
with each quick click of fingers.
Sunlight falls through your hair;
makes even the robins jealous.
The air, a riverboat of floribunda, floats
before those lingering by the fountain,
a summer the stars remember what
they left in this city, why they color
night's solitude and you awakening geranium,
cuckoo and water lily.

IV
POEMS TO LEAVE UNDER A TREE

Barnacle

Since the day was a buoy on a fogless horizon,
    spinning off the blue jay's wing,
he thought it was time to sweep
    the sandfleas from his rocky house.
The tide was so far out it was
    a painting of First People's village.
The sun was rising over Mount Takoma
    like a crab over the labyrinth,
pincer prancing from island to island.
    The waters of Puget Sound
were as flat as a flounder's eye.
    This was why the sun
took a nap before making its steep climb
    up the Chilkat blanket sky
to the opening of the moon's cave.
    O, he had heard his grandfather
tell the story of sun's journey all right,
    that its path was not for him.
It was no worry, nor did he lose
    footing even once, remembering
it was more fun kicking sand in the dark,
    riding the next crest to what
surprises in the surf. Besides, for several
    waves he was as dizzy as the air.
He could feel his eyebrows dry in the heat,
    but not too dry or saltless.
From each point where the snipe takes a new
    direction and breath comes, the sun's
yellow tracks leave incandescent spots crossing
    Elliot Bay on the way to the Ho-Had-Huns
and Northwest coast that is a tail of Killer Whale's.
    The arc and fall of the orange star
was as quiet as the great blue heron,
    waiting like a totem for a perch.
He could feel Yellow Face's drumbeats roll
    down his toes like the moment
before a storm, when thunder would almost unmoor
    his home, lightning strike his name
to flakes whistling in the wind. But then
    he glowed like the eel when the storm
ran back to its own beginning. He would
    shake with wonder because he was
in his shell and light's nimble finger.
    When the surf began to build

like hills, then mountains, and slap and pound
    against his house, all his fingers
flowered in the spray to dance with kelp
    and herring gulls, churning smoother circles
through whatever lands as the past, feeds
    the hunger of the future, and for the medicine
pouring from the hollows of his cousins,
    the sand dollars.

Rufous Hummingbird

You almost trip as you hear
it dart past the azalea shrubs
to the solitary fox-glove.
It wears the colors of the sky
while the season snatches another wing.

Immersed in the greenbean's
swift phrase, it also has a bill
for honeysuckle and apple.
Such plucky, sparse flights of this
green and red-throated spool

of dashing light sets you in a body
so small and nimble you could walk
in a space where nerves dance on an earth
clover-patched and leaf-stalked.
Even rock-fence lichen float down this stream.

December Rose

Bold stem,
yellow as cold,
more sinewy than a bow,
you stay as ancient as the crow,
rain's stone.

The Salmon

Mother of salt and slate,
foam and storm, eye of columbine;
sea flower carried by our shadow people
in a canoe on a horizon of mud and slime,
under the forest floor;

mixer of scale, bone, and blood,
nose of Thunderbird who answered her wave
as it passed our rainbow mountain;
mother of calm and deliverance,
the tongue's drum from the cliff.

High above the raven valleys
near the sea, dream fox
with the thread of the current in its mouth
touches the Elwha River twice
as she nestles her eggs in the gravel.
The roots of the wind's hair
builds the birth cradle out of moon and tide.

Salmon Woman, a streaky
thrust at fertility, edges like Dawnmaker
up the slope, the thinning trail of the river.
Fever rattle of joy and tenacity,
gills bellow fullness and emptiness:
the songs of grandmothers
around Hadlock village fires that wove
our daughters into blankets and water dreamers.

North Rain

Its topaz cuts quicken
 the forsythia
 like the thunder
driving the geese south.

The elm is pared to
 the spirit;
 the earth
quakes with abandoned webs.

Each dances for the other,
 the wind,
 pierced notes,
the taut grip, grey and umber.

Michigan Storm

August night has the taste and smell of thunder;
the heart bolts in the cross-currents.
The wind sprints north and south,
east and west like a buffalo herd.
A white buffalo leads them
through the torrent of rain and cleavage—
it returns the storm to the womb,
the country's Plains, open as the sea.

Hello, goodbye, geraniums uptwisted as the sky,
their zig-zag dance a parody of night.
I clap when they clap, sing when they sing,
step in their tracks arching the hollows;
will not leave the path until my heart
is as wave-formed as the cloud-rugs,
stitched and unstitched on thunder's loom.

Past midnight the horizon sparks like flint;
the soul whistles in dark deliverance.
Moon and stars fill the greenhouse blaze
burning out and down to thunder ashes.
This story's blood shines gold and blue on the grass.
The herd gallops more in canyon than mountain;
maples shimmer but with no commitment to the wind.

Three Rounds on the Hill of Winter

The snow,
a surface thin as paper,
layers the hours.
In the sky
are islands in suspension,
gray and white,
a clan of airpods drifting from one
reservation to the next.

The wind
moves as the Oregon juncos scratching
round the ice.

The blue
opens its window all the way
to the sea, plants your feet on the path
to the highest Salish mountain
on the wingbeat of eagles. Grandfather
Yellow Eyes shows how to embrace
what the earth ciders.

The half moon
triggers a red memory to speak
with the madrona-tree, the hillside,
the rest of the river tribe.

The sun,
holding my shadow, casts life
into a thicker skin,
my blood into a birthing leapfrog,
then like the most Northwestern
split light, it rolls backwards
and falls like a hoop
in the weeds.

Poem to Leave Under a Tree

A few Canadian geese slant
across the sky but no snow
slips off the branches
from the honking.

They breathe a blue
as subterranean as the pond
the spruce drink. Fueled by
Lake Michigan air I am
ready to take any turn
the sun takes, leap
with red intent if one drunk
snowdrop animates more
than the tombs in the cemetery.

I am then sure to return
home and find a guardian spirit
drew song sparrows on my window,
so I might sleep in a cave
as deep orange as the monarch
butterfly, winter's mummy,
my friend, nothingness's
corolla alchemist.

Coastal Storm
(for Sue)

The sun teeters vertical on the marginal;
the wind and rain catapult the wave
up and over the other side of the dune.

Chasing bubbles of sea-scum down the beach
we spot an oil-slicked common murre,
pretending to hide in a clump of eelgrass.

I catch the bird so we can take it to a vet,
though it already looks a burr of death.
Off the road the fields shadow-pace the marsh hawks.

The hawks, earth-hatched for the spirals of air,
hovered in the wake of the sea-fed moon,
banked to where the crest-cradled dawn rises.

V
MOON STORIES

The Moon Stories are in memory of Mrs. Annie Patsy Duncan, my Great-Aunt, and her father, Young Patsy. Young Patsy had two "Indian names" and one was Niatum. My Great-Aunt honored me with the gift of this name in 1971. In gratitude and with respect to her father's lineage and traditions, soon after I made it legally my last name.

Moon of Crackling Branches

This gray wolf and clan miss
the central turn of the moon
so they roam all winter across
the body of the land. They look
always to the ground; stars
have not blessed them with one song.
Days and nights have been so cold
their coats are packed with pine
needles, mud burrs, and snow clots.
Without a catch for days, their
shadows are thin branches
of hemlock boughs. Crystal faces of their
grandparents drift on and on through
our sleep like the blizzard.

When they quit calling their
brothers and sisters to keep moving
and singing like the river,
the ice, the snow, the dream,
we will lose a shield
and most of our spirit.

Moon of Deep Snow

Above the snow tracks
a sparrow splashes with his eyes
through the blue rivulets,
an opaque melt but as real
as our homage to uncertainty.

Sparrow promises to sing
of first witnessing frost's
slip from the field,
the sun reaching the alder
and poplar's deep ravine,
the slant green notes composed.

Dark as afternoon,
a bush of holly berries
draws the rest
of the robin clan
to the buoyant branch.

We hear for a moment
the animals on the early
morning path linger in the maples
before we enter the fern
gates with the tribe.

Exiting into the street
a purple crocus springs
us into a prism of almosts.
Lazily, we breathe the ocher
light, fold back the vines,
hope the blossom will dance
with what the moon brings.

Moon of Chinook Winds

I

The willow's ancient companion,
a crow preens himself in the sun,
winters like fog's clan,
the snow retreating toward the river.
Is he my grandfather?

II

The day flows steady as volcanic ash.
I stare at the river and rocks
speckled with the sharp eyes of ice.
The wren family skittering toward
tall grass knows where to rest,
why don't I and the winds?

III

The woman who keeps my blood a shield,
the friends awaiting my return to Seattle,
let me sink into the Hoko's reflection
like a trout. An empty canoe in water's web,
my soul bounces in the current.

IV

Grandfather, Great-Uncle Joe,
I chant for your stories older than the mountains:
as Raven asks Killer Whale,
is to swim the river of our sacred mountain
the medicine to cool my rage and fear?

V

When the Moon of Chinook Winds
tramples through what is left of the red fir
forest like a grizzly for the last night,
I will sleep between the crow's
lean shadow and the wolf's.

Moon of Flowers
(for Jan, Panos, and Marilyn)

The deer at Hurricane Ridge
cross a canyon of the moon's.
Our friends watch the tips of their tails
vanish, black as our evening steps.

This spring night the changes
are to learn the ways to follow
the wind's season, the motions
and stillness of the yellow violet.

So the next time my love drops her
wish into my hand, each color growing
in the meadow of her eyes
will keep me dancing to the edge.

Wandering like the blind through the garden,
the labyrinth of speech, we claim nothing
from the stars, only give
our rhythms to the sky.

Awaking next morning we see if what
blossomed the night before eases
the fracture of our nomadic isolation,
shows the swallows' green chorus wasn't a lie.

Moon of Ripe Berries

Huckleberries, as sun-glazed as the Cascade mountains,
nearly drop into our hands when we jump a fallen cedar.

They are the light children of stump
and rain, one summer gift.

Snoqualmie Falls turns the bear tracks into fish bone,
the swallows flight into mist.

Hidden, tricky, time's backwards thief,
never really still, here nor there, a blue jay

hops at the chance to steal our bread
our drink, our humor.

Pebbles roll, pass over and under the stars,
the wild primroses along the cliff path.

Feasting on what red caps the crows ignored,
we rise to step under the falls,

cool off with the spray and pool water.
Our memories open like wings.

Moon of Dry Grass

I

Beyond the range of the dissonant city,
I kneel to drink tahoma water,
search for Old Patsy's longhouse,
the remains of his last potlatch.

Beyond the white fir fire, a brown bear
lopes through the brush of the far
ravine's lichen-aired noon. Has he spotted
a sweet hive or trampled away to die?

II

Buzzing in blind dives about my face,
a mosquito chooses to dance
than take a chance of losing its connection.

With the unearthed discovery in the form
of a paddle, I rest like a branch
from the Sitka spruce, to keep
the blood and crest of this man's heart.

Moon Of Harvest

The crack and scrape of tiny legends
begin to fall, build yellow mounds.
The maple leaves ignite the evening;
give what thunders through the maze,
the bats' ease in moonless umbra.

Moon of Frost's Return

I

A coyote howl adds a lingering irony
to the Elwha River ghosts,
the red-cedar fisherman too hard-grained
as the lavas at Mats Mats Bay
to stay settled in this field of poetry,
too buried under mudslides to be reached
with a watch or car. Like the thunder
in the hills, a wind rolls off a peak;
carries the colors of the alpine sky
over the fir, hemlock, pine, and maple,
zig-zagging a trail to Port Angeles.

II

On the lower slopes of Memp-ch-ton,
the cumulus clouds blacken the willow
branches; the day's images float away
with the river down the mountain.
For the joke in the move, the wind
raises its pitch one green octave above
the chickadee confronting the freeze,
myself growing thinner than the marmot tracks
through snow, mud, and rain.

A storm pulls in its wings from the coast,
changes my guess at the right direction
of my ancestors' oldest trail home,
the one now chosen even with its sudden
shifts in direction and what is there.
Like the chickadee singing a song
to the branch burdened with much snow,
I put my beak to the wind.

Moon of Winter

I camp near the marsh, once the longhouse site
of Shupald, Old Patsy, my great-great grandfather,
now home to mallard and coot, muskrat
and cat-tail rush. Waves strike driftwood
and rocks and tumble down shore.
Small birds fly to roost in the red
and yellow cedars. The dark
is a shaker of sparks from the fire.
I sit and wait the return of my tamahnous.
When and if it airs its wobbly mask
failures and false promises will be tossed
like gambling sticks in the sand
the way the sea carves its mosaic on all
it touches, then leaves behind.

On this beach for generations my mother's
family picked chokecherries, gooseberries,
baked salmon, steamed clam and oyster and mussel,
sang to their dead and newborn,
deer and bear, moon, and especially, the sun.
Free from Seattle's grid I come back
to learn the songs of my family
and the seven Klallam brothers who lived
in villages surrounding Hadlock Bay.

O to live with wind and confusion, ice and disease,
stop the drum of Raven's mockeries!

Notes

Chi-ah-ya-og – Ojibwa name for "the elders."

Ho-Had-Huns – Nisqually name for the Olympic Mountains.

Mount Takoma – Coast Salish tribal name for Mount Rainier.

Nishnaabeg – Name the Ojibwa use for themselves (plural).

Grizzly Bear Stars – what some Salish tribes call "the Big Dipper."

Lake Duwamish – probably the Duwamish name for Lake Washington.

Oatsa is the author's maternal great grandmother's Indian name and Niatum is his maternal great grandfather's Indian name.

White Trail in the Sky – Salish for "the Milky Way."

Moon Names

Moon of Crackling Branches: (Lummi) January

Moon of Deep Snow: (Lummi) February

Moon of Chinook Winds: (Lummi) March

Moon of Flowers: (Lummi) May

Moon of Ripe Berries: (Lummi) July

Moon of Dry Grass: (Lummi) August

Moon of Harvest: (Lummi) September

Moon of Frost's Return: (Lummi) November

Moon of Winter: (Lummi) December